This marriage study series is pure Focus on the Family—
reliable, biblically sound and dedicated to reestablishing family values
in today's society. This series will no doubt help a multitude of couples
strengthen their relationship, not only with each other,
but also with God, the *creator* of marriage itself.

Bruce Wilkinson

Author, The BreakThrough Series: *The Prayer of Jabez,
Secrets of the Vine* and *A Life God Rewards*

In this era of such need, Dr. Dobson's team has produced solid,
helpful materials about Christian marriage. Even if they have been
through marriage studies before, every couple—married or engaged—
will benefit from this foundational study of life together. Thanks to
Focus on the Family for helping set us straight in this top priority.

Charles W. Colson

Chairman, Prison Fellowship Ministries

In my 31 years as a pastor, I've officiated at hundreds of weddings.
Unfortunately, many of those unions failed. I only wish the *Focus on the
Family Marriage Series* had been available to me during those years.
What a marvelous tool you as pastors and Christian leaders have
at your disposal. I encourage you to use it to assist those you
serve in building successful, healthy marriages.

H. B. London, Jr.

Vice President, Ministry Outreach/Pastoral Ministries
Focus on the Family

Looking for a prescription for a better marriage?
You'll enjoy this timely and practical series!

Dr. Kevin Leman

Author, *Sheet Music: Uncovering the Secrets of
Sexual Intimacy in Marriage*

The *Focus on the Family Marriage Series* is successful because it shifts
the focus from how to fix or strengthen a marriage to *who* can do it.
Through this study you will learn that a blessed marriage will be the
happy by-product of a closer relationship with the *creator* of marriage.

Lisa Whelchel

Author, *Creative Correction* and
The Facts of Life and Other Lessons My Father Taught Me

In a day and age where the covenant of marriage is so quickly tossed
aside in the name of incompatibility and irreconcilable differences, a
marriage Bible study that is both inspirational and practical is desperately
needed. The *Focus on the Family Marriage Series* is what couples are seeking.
I give my highest recommendation to this Bible study series that has the
potential to dramatically impact and improve marriages today. Marriage
is not so much about finding the right partner as it is about being the
right partner. These studies give wonderful biblical teachings for
helping those who want to learn the beautiful art of being and
becoming all that God intends in their marriage.

Lysa TerKeurst

President, Proverbs 31 Ministries
Author, *Capture His Heart* and *Capture Her Heart*

focus on the family® marriage series

the masterpiece *marriage*

Gospel Light

Gospel Light is an evangelical Christian publisher dedicated to serving the local church. We believe God's vision for Gospel Light is to provide church leaders with biblical, user-friendly materials that will help them evangelize, disciple and minister to children, youth and families.

It is our prayer that this Gospel Light resource will help you discover biblical truth for your own life and help you minister to others. May God richly bless you.

For a free catalog of resources from Gospel Light, please call your Christian supplier or contact us at 1-800-4-GOSPEL *or* www.gospellight.com

PUBLISHING STAFF
William T. Greig, Chairman
Kyle Duncan, Publisher
Dr. Elmer L. Towns, Senior Consulting Publisher
Pam Weston, Senior Editor
Patti Pennington Virtue, Associate Editor
Hilary Young, Editorial Assistant
Kathryn T. Schuh, Editorial Assistant
Bayard Taylor, M.Div., Senior Editor, Biblical and Theological Issues
Samantha A. Hsu, Cover and Internal Designer
Christi Goeser, Contributing Writer

table of contents

foreword

The most urgent mission field on Earth is not across the sea or even across the street—it's right where you live: in your home and family. Jesus' last instruction was to "make disciples of all nations" (Matthew 28:19). At the thought of this command, our eyes look across the world for our work field. That's not bad; it's just not *all*. God intended the home to be the first place of Christian discipleship and growth (see Deuteronomy 6:4-8). Our family members must be the *first* ones we reach out to in word and example with the gospel of the Lord Jesus Christ, and the fundamental way in which this occurs is through the marriage relationship.

Divorce, blended families, the breakdown of communication and the complexities of daily life are taking a devastating toll on the God-ordained institutions of marriage and family. We do not need to look hard or search far for evidence that even Christian marriages and families are also in a desperate state. In response to the need to build strong Christ-centered marriages and families, this series was developed.

Focus on the Family is well known and respected worldwide for its stead-fast dedication to preserving the sanctity of marriage and family life. I can think of no better partnership than the one formed by Focus on the Family and Gospel Light to produce the *Focus on the Family Marriage Series*. This series is well-written, biblically sound and right on target for guiding couples to explore the foundation God has laid for marriage and to see Him as the role model for the perfect spouse. Through these studies, seeds will be planted that will germinate in your heart and mind for many years to come.

In our practical, bottom-line culture, we often want to jump over the *why* and get straight to the *what*. We think that by *doing* the six steps or *learning* the five ways, we will reach the goal. But deep-rooted growth is slower and more purposeful and begins with a well-grounded understanding of God's divine design. Knowing why marriage exists is crucial to making the how-tos more effective. Marriage is a gift from God, a unique and distinct covenant relationship through which His glory and goodness can resonate, and it is only through knowing the architect and His plan that we will build our marriage on the surest foundation.

God created marriage; He has a specific purpose for it, and He is committed to filling with fresh life and renewed strength each union yielded to Him. God wants to gather the hearts of every couple together, unite them in love and walk them to the finish line—all in His great grace and goodness.

May God, in His grace, lead you into His truth, strengthening your lives and your marriage.

Gary T. Smalley
Founder and Chairman of the Board
Smalley Relationship Center

introduction

*At the beginning of creation God "made them male and female." "For this
reason a man will leave his father and mother and be united to his wife,
and the two will become one flesh." So they are no longer two, but one.*
Mark 10:6-8

The Masterpiece Marriage can be used in a variety of situations, including
small-group Bible studies, Sunday School classes or counseling or mentoring situations. An individual couple can also use this book as an at-home
marriage-building study.

Each of the four sessions contains four main components.

Session Overview

Tilling the Ground
This is an introduction to the topic being discussed—commentary and questions to direct your thoughts toward the main idea of the session.

Planting the Seed
This is the Bible study portion in which you will read Scripture and answer
questions to help discover lasting truths from God's Word.

Watering the Hope
This is a time for discussion and prayer. Whether you are using the study at
home as a couple, in a small group or in a classroom setting, talking about
the lesson with your spouse is a great way to solidify the truth and plant it
deeply into your hearts.

Harvesting the Fruit
As a point of action, this portion of the session offers suggestions on putting
the truth of the Word into action in your marriage relationship.

Suggestions for Individual Couple Study

There are at least three options for using this study as a couple.

- It may be used as a devotional study that each spouse would study individually through the week; then on a specified day, come together and discuss what you have learned and how to apply it to your marriage.
- You might choose to study one session together in an evening and then work on the application activities during the rest of the week.
- Because of the short length of this study, it is a great resource for a weekend retreat. Take a trip away for the weekend, and study each session together, interspersed with your favorite leisure activities.

Suggestions for Group Study

There are many ways that this study can be used in a group situation. The most common way is in a small-group Bible study format. However, it can also be used in an adult Sunday School class. However you choose to use it, there are some general guidelines to follow for group study.

- Keep the group small—five to six couples is probably the maximum.
- Ask couples to commit to regular attendance for the four weeks of the study. Regular attendance is a key to building relationships and trust in a group.
- Encourage participants *not* to share anything of a personal or potentially embarrassing nature without first asking the spouse's permission.
- Whatever is discussed in the group meetings is to be held in strictest confidence among group members only.

There are additional leader helps in the back of this book and in *The Focus on the Family Marriage Ministry Guide*.

Suggestions for Mentoring or Counseling Relationships

This study also lends itself for use in relationships where one couple mentors or counsels another couple.

- A mentoring relationship could be arranged through a system set up by a church or ministry: A couple that has been married for several years is assigned to meet on a regular basis with a younger couple.
- A less formal way to start a mentoring relationship is for a younger couple to take the initiative and approach a couple that exemplify a mature, godly marriage and ask them to meet with them on a regular basis. Or the reverse might be a mature couple that approaches a younger couple to begin a mentoring relationship.
- When asked to mentor, some might shy away and think that they could never do that, knowing that their own marriage is less than perfect. But just as we are to disciple new believers, we must learn to disciple married couples to strengthen marriages in this difficult world. The Lord has promised to be "with you always" (Matthew 28:20).
- Before you begin to mentor a couple, first complete the study yourselves. This will serve to strengthen your own marriage and prepare you for leading another couple.
- Be prepared to learn as much or more than the couple(s) you will mentor.

There are additional helps for mentoring relationships in *The Focus on the Family Marriage Ministry Guide.*

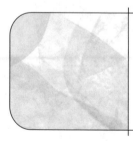

The Focus on the Family Marriage Series *is based on Al Janssen's* The Marriage Masterpiece *(Wheaton, IL: Tyndale House Publishers, 2001), an insightful look at what marriage can—and should—be. In this study, we are pleased to lead you through the wonderful journey of discovering the joy in your marriage that God wants you to experience!*

great expectations

So God created man in his own image, in the image of God
he created him; male and female he created them.
Genesis 1:27

Imagine that you are planning a trip from your home to the North Pole. First, you dust off your gear and get it ready. Then you purchase additional supplies, making sure to run through your checklist several times to be sure that you have everything you need. Finally, you are ready to embark on your journey.

Now imagine that the only flaw in your carefully packed gear is a faulty compass which leads you in a direction just one degree off your intended course. At first there would not be any noticeable error; you would continue your route and enjoy the scenery. Eventually, though, you would realize that your destination is not in sight and that your imperfect compass reading had led you to another place—one you hadn't planned on visiting!

In some ways our lives, and particularly our marriage relationships, can experience a similar problem. We start off running with what seems to be calculated perfection. We have all the right tools, know all the right lingo and begin the journey with decided confidence and boundless energy. Then somewhere along the line we find ourselves off course, and we wonder what happened. We aren't where we thought we'd be—and we don't know why.

Great marriages start by discovering God's plan.

- Why did God create marriage?
- What is this covenant relationship all about?
- What is the final destination for a husband and wife?

By defining our expectations for a marriage relationship, allowing God to fine tune our desires to His, harmonizing with His purposes and will, not only can we arrive at the right place, but we can also enjoy the trip!

1. As you were growing up, what was your general opinion of marriage?

2. Before you were married, what did you expect your marriage would be like?

3. After you were married, how did your expectations change?

4. How did your expectations meet with your experience?

5. In your opinion, what is the ultimate purpose, or the final destination, for marriage?

6. From your answers above, identify your top three marriage expectations.

7. What would you say your spouse's top three marriage expectations might be?

Most likely, none of the expectations you listed are unrealistic. But if we want to comprehend the true purpose of something, why it was invented, what we can expect it to do and how it best works, we first should look at the inventor. Likewise, if we want to understand the purpose of marriage—its divine design—then we need to go to the one who designed it: God!

planting the seed

Expectation—Hope on a Rope

Expectation is like a compass that determines how we address the day-to-day choices of life and, ultimately, which direction we are walking. The Hebrew word for "expectation" is *tiqvah*, which is also translated "hope." It literally means "something yearned for; something for which one waits." Interestingly, the original meaning comes from a word that means "to stretch like a rope."[1]

8. What does the "scarlet cord" (or "rope," depending on your Bible translation) in Joshua 2:17-21 remind you of? (See also Exodus 12:22-23; 1 Corinthians 5:7; 1 Peter 1:19.)

Rahab's scarlet rope was her hope—her anticipation of salvation in the face of destruction. She hung that cord—*tiqvah*—in her window, believing that God would deliver her and her family, and He did.

In the New Testament, the word translated either "expectation" or "hope" means "a confident expectation based upon solid certainty."[2] Biblical hope is much more than wishful thinking; it is a rope attached to a stake that's been driven into the rock—a stand of faith that finds its strength in the promise giver. We can have strong hope and we can expect good things because God *is* our hope!

9. What do each of the following verses say about hope?

Psalm 71:5

Proverbs 23:18

Jeremiah 29:11

Romans 15:13

Colossians 1:27

Hebrews 10:23

10. From these Scriptures, how would you define hope?

11. How should hope affect your life?

Okay, okay—you're probably thinking, *What in the world does this have to do with marriage?* Well, not only does the Bible have much to say about our expectations, but also it speaks to the primary topic at hand: the *why* of marriage. Let's discover God's expectation for this amazing union.

A Glimpse of Glory

The Bible has a lot to say about marriage—its purpose and its destination. As you work through this section, think about God's design for the marriage relationship.

Genesis 1—2 reveals God as the creator of the world and everything in it. Read the first two chapters of Genesis; then reread the verses as directed and answer the questions for each.

12. According to Genesis 1:3,6,9,14,20,24, how did God create the things listed in these verses?

13. According to Genesis 2:7, what is different about the way God created man?

14. What does the fact that God personally made the first man and the first woman, using His own hands to form them and breathing His very life into them, say to you about the uniqueness of you and your spouse?

It is often said that art reflects life. This is true about the world around us and is also true about God. His creation is an expression of His heart—and reveals something about who He is.

15. How do the following verses underscore the point that creation reveals God?

Psalm 19:1-4

Romans 1:20

We've noted that, of all God's creation, humankind is His crowning achievement—His most valued handiwork. Because humans were made alive by God's Spirit, we are spiritual beings with the ability to relate to God like no other part of creation can.

We hear the pleasure of God as each layer of creation is brought forth in precision and beauty—light, sky, land, stars, plants and animals: "God saw that it was good" (Genesis 1:4,9,12,18,21,25). But after He made man, His joy was doubly evident: "God saw all that he had made, and it was very good" (Genesis 1:31).

It's a Fact!	*In the original account of creation from Genesis 1—2,* adam *is not just the personal name for the man, Adam, but it can also mean "human being" or "humankind," which clearly includes both male and female people.*

We have seen from the Bible that all of God's creation is a reflection of who He is, a signpost and a testimony to His great glory, wisdom and creativity. Now consider His apex creation: both Adam *and* Eve. They were so uniquely designed that they, when rightly united, could better testify to the nature of God than the most perfect sunrise or the most striking mountain skyline.

Both the man and the woman are needed to reveal the true nature of God. The ultimate goal of marriage—God's expectation for it—is the reflection of His image. Although our human sinfulness disallows the full character of His glory to be revealed, as husband and wife we are the most suited to exemplify the One who made us (even in light of our apparent depravity).

16. How might John 13:34-35 and 17:23 relate to unity in marriage as a reflection of the image of God?

Through the union of marriage, we can reflect a glimpse of the glory of God to the world around us. This is our brightest hope and our greatest expectation: to bring the message of God's love and redemption to the world. Jesus Himself said that it was through our love and through our unity that the world would be drawn to Him. We most often assume that this love and unity primarily occurs in our daily relationship with others. Without a doubt it does, but when you think about the heart of God revealed through His creation of the world and of mankind, where is the first picture of true unity? It is in the creation of the mankind—male and female. God wants love and unity expressed most fully in the unique, divine relationship between a man and a woman that we call marriage.

Marriage is all about oneness—beginning when God removed Adam's rib to form Eve and then gave Eve to Adam so that they could become one flesh again. This oneness is not an end in and of itself, however, and this is where our expectations come in.

When we expect that the primary purpose of marriage is self-fulfillment and personal happiness, we miss its higher purpose and set ourselves up for disappointment and heartache. Without a doubt, marriage is a place of deep intimacy and joy—unlike any other relationship we can enjoy here on Earth. Yet this fulfillment and joy, this security and companionship, are merely the by-products of marriage's highest purpose: oneness that reflects the oneness of God Himself, revealing His desire to be one with us.

17. What do the following verses say about God's purpose for marriage?

Matthew 19:4-6

Ephesians 5:31-32

It is God's expectation that through the love shared by a husband and wife, both would better understand—and demonstrate to the world—their Father's love for them. Marriage, like all other creation, is meant to draw our eyes to God.

 watering the hope

Take some time to reflect on what you've learned about God's expectations for marriage.

18. Review the expectations you listed at the beginning of this session. In light of what has been shared, have your expectations of what marriage is all about changed at all? How?

19. Do you agree that the highest purpose of marriage is the reflection of God's glory? Why or why not?

20. What expectations might strengthen a marriage relationship?

21. How might seeking God's expectations for your marriage actually lead to greater self-fulfillment?

Often, too much emphasis is placed on romantic feelings of love. When feelings are gone, people assume that the love is gone too and thus look for it elsewhere.

22. How can a better understanding of God's expectation for marriage give couples a strong point of hope for their relationships?

harvesting the fruit

The biblical basis for marriage is relationship between a husband and wife that leads both their hearts to deeper communion with God. We must realign our hearts to the biblical expectations.

- God created marriage.
- God gave marriage a divine purpose and goal.
- God meant marriage to be a reflection of the oneness He desires to have with us.

Plan a specific time in the next week during which you will review the vows you made at your wedding.

23. What did you promise to each other?

24. What do you expect from each other in light of the vows you made?

25. How does your marriage relationship reflect something of God's nature and/or give glory to Him?

26. What is one attitude or action that you need to change in order to begin to fulfill God's purpose for your marriage?

Pray together that God continues to open your eyes to His divine design for your marriage. Ask Him for His guidance and blessing to help you align your own expectations for marriage to His.

Notes
1. Jack W. Hayford, ed., *Hayford's Bible Handbook* (Nashville, TN: Thomas Nelson, 1995), s.v. "hope."
2. Ibid.

the divine *triangle*

*For this reason a man will leave his father and mother and be united
to his wife, and they will become one flesh. The man and his wife
were both naked, and they felt no shame.*

Genesis 2:24-25

You have probably heard the saying, Two's company; three's a crowd. This may be true in some situations but not in a marriage! In a marriage relationship that works the way God designed, two can be difficult, but three is truly divine. True happiness comes from the three-way relationship between a man, a woman and God. Our highest fulfillment in marriage comes when God is invited not only to be a part of the ceremony but also to be the ever-present, all-sustaining strength of the relationship.

Have you ever watched someone braid a rope? Loose fibers are twisted together in an endless stream of bending and stretching. The end result: one cord whose strength far surpasses the individual strands. Two strands alone, even if twisted with considerable force, will eventually break or unravel, but three strands can be woven into something remarkably strong and durable. In much the same way, you and your spouse are unique strands, each bringing to your relationship the various strengths and giftings God gave you. With God as the third strand in the cord of your marriage, it will be even stronger than two alone.

Ecclesiastes 4:12 verifies what we know to be true: "A cord of three strands is not easily broken." We want to have a strong marriage. We want to rest confidently in the durability of our relationship. How can we do this? One way is to strengthen the individual strands and then submit them in committed faith to the One who holds all things together.

1. In the past week how have you and your spouse witnessed the truth that "a cord of three strands is not easily broken"?

2. In what way have you experienced the fraying, unraveling or even breaking of your cord?

In the Beginning

Take a moment to consider the life Adam and Eve had. Adam, created by the hand and breath of God (see Genesis 2:7), is placed in the Garden of Eden and given the charge to "work it and take care of it" (v. 15). Walking through the pristine beauty of the newly created world, naming the animals, talking daily with God, living free from the harness of sin or selfishness, Adam had a good life! But it was not enough; God had more in mind.

3. What did God say about Adam's state of singleness in Genesis 2:18?

4. How did God answer this need in verses 21-22?

5. How does the fact that God chose to create Eve out of Adam's own rib (see v. 22), instead of by His word or from the dust of the ground, point to God's purpose for marriage?

6. Since Adam and Eve did not have earthly parents, what is significant about the instruction given in Genesis 2:24? What does this statement underscore about the fundamental structure of marriage?

Jesus refers to Genesis 2:24-25 as the foundational point for understanding God's intent for marriage. Read Matthew 19:4-6. Think about the phrase "what God has joined together." Marriage is much more than two people choosing to share a last name and a bank account. It is a divine relationship where God Himself knits a man and a woman together for the purpose of being one. In God's eyes, it is a permanent bonding of lives.

7. In what ways have you seen God working in your marriage to bring you and your spouse closer together?

God obviously felt that man needed woman, that the charge to tend the garden would be better done with the aid of another, so He gave Eve to Adam. This isn't to say that single people are somehow incomplete, but it does point to the truth that God's design for the fullest opportunity for the expression of His glory is to be in the joining of a man and a woman in marriage. With His ongoing guidance and presence, they will grow together and reveal His image to the world around them. With God as the initiator and sustainer of their relationship, Adam and Eve would not only care for the world God made but enjoy it as well. But it takes all three to make this happen: the man, the woman *and* God.

Strengthening the Strands

If our individual lives are strong and healthy, then we are more likely to enjoy a strong and healthy marriage. The strength of the threefold cord is dependent upon each strand. This doesn't imply that a "perfect" husband and a "perfect" wife equal a perfect marriage, or that if you and your spouse aren't strong strands, then your marriage is bound to unravel. What is does mean is that as each one seeks the Lord, surrendering his or her own life to His ever-refining mercy, the cord becomes more and more about Him, and more and more durable and secure.

God's grace is only seen when we face our complete inadequacy and ask for His power to do what we are powerless to do for ourselves. It is one's personal commitment to Christ, to a consistent devotional life and to ongoing surrender to one's spouse that makes marriage a divine triangle of blessing.

Great Marriages Begin with Personal Commitments to Jesus Christ

Jesus Christ is the only door to a personal relationship with God. When we surrender our lives to His lordship, He restores us to right relationships with Him. This paves the way to right relationships with others.

8. Read and summarize Romans 3:23.

Salvation begins by understanding that we have sinned and fallen far short of God's perfect plan for our lives. We are lost in our own rebellion and cannot save ourselves no matter how hard we try.

9. What does Romans 6:23 say about the result of sin and what God offers to us?

The good news is that God sent His only Son, Jesus Christ, to provide us with complete redemption from sin. Jesus' sinless life and His death for our sins provide salvation for all who will believe: "For God so loved the world that he gave his one and only Son, that whoever believes in him shall not perish but have eternal life" (John 3:16).

10. What does Romans 10:9-13 say about how to express belief in Jesus?

Because salvation is a gift offered by our gracious God, our only response is to graciously receive it.

11. Can you say with confidence that Jesus is your Lord?

☐ Yes   ☐ No

12. Describe your salvation experience.

If you have never accepted Jesus Christ as Savior, won't you consider receiving Him by faith right now? The Bible is clear: When we come to the Lord, He will receive us. Take a moment and consider the truths that have been discussed here and what you must do in response.

Great Marriages Are Strengthened by Consistent Personal Devotion

A commitment to Christ must be encouraged daily through good devotional habits that include Bible reading, prayer and fellowship with other believers.

13. What do Romans 15:4 and 2 Timothy 3:16-17 say about the purpose for reading God's Word?

14. What does Philippians 4:6-7 tell you about the result of prayer?

15. According to Hebrews 10:24-25, why is it important to meet together with other Christians?

16. Which of these three spiritual habits are you presently practicing on a regular basis?

Which do you need to add to your daily activities?

Great Marriages Endure Through Ongoing Personal Submission

Keeping your personal relationship with Christ strong and ever growing will afford you the grace and strength needed to pour yourself into the life of your spouse. Individual submission to God and then to each other is the secret to enjoying this divine triangle.

Ephesians 5:21-33 provides the guidelines for submission to one another.

17. What does it mean to "submit to one another out of reverence for Christ" (v. 21)?

18. In your marriage, is there a mutual submission to each other because of your personal commitments to God? Give a recent example of how you have shown submission to your spouse.

How has your spouse recently shown submission to you?

How have you recently shown submission to God?

19. How has your marriage been affected by not submitting to one another out of reverence for Christ?

20. In Ephesians 5:22-24, what specifically is the wife told to do? What is the model of submission used in these verses?

21. What does submission mean to you?

Is a wife's submission license for her husband to become the dictator of the relationship? Explain your answer.

In an act of faith and trust, wives submit to their husbands. Because of the mutual submission first to the Lord and then to each other, a wife voluntarily takes a place under the shelter of the husband, not as an inferior, but as a suitable helper.

22. As you read Ephesians 5:25-28, note verse by verse the manner in which the husband is to respond to his wife.

Verse 25

Verse 26

Verse 27

Verse 28

The husband responds to the wife's submission, not by asserting his authority and lording over her, but by laying down his life for her, committing himself fully to her well-being and success.

23. Summarize Ephesians 5:29-33.

24. In what ways is Christ's love reflected to others through your marriage?

Marriage is meant to be an echo of an even greater relationship that exists between Christ and the Church. It is the oneness seen in a healthy marriage that offers a glimpse to the world around us of the ultimate oneness of the Lord and His Bride, the Church. When marriage is founded upon these truths, it can accomplish God's greater purpose, revealing through the union a picture of what it means to be one with God.

watering the hope

Marriage is meant to be a divine triangle reflecting the grace and glory of God: a man and a woman bound together by the very life of God Himself. It is a unique and distinct relationship created and sustained by the Spirit of the Lord.

25. (For wives) How do you live out the command to submit to your husband? What specific actions should you take on a daily and weekly basis to demonstrate your respect (see Ephesians 5:33) for him?

Daily	Weekly

26. (For husbands) How do you live out the command to love your wife as "Christ loved the church" (v. 25)? What specific actions should you take on a daily and weekly basis to demonstrate your love for her?

Daily	Weekly

harvesting the fruit

A husband and wife have the divine opportunity and calling to show forth the nature of God in a unique and distinct way. Surrendering to God's design for marriage means that we are no longer focused on finding personal happiness. Instead, we turn our gaze upon the One who is both our desire and its fulfillment. Joined in marriage, united by God's Spirit, a husband and wife are truly free to honor God and each other.

27. Describe the first time you met your spouse.

28. What did you like most about your spouse when you met?

29. Was there a specific moment when you knew that he or she was the person with whom you wanted to share the rest of your life?

30. Looking back, describe how God worked in your lives to bring you together.

31. In what ways has your marriage been a two-person relationship?

32. In what ways might it be a one-person relationship?

33. What areas need to be brought back to the Lord, inviting Him to weave His grace and joy back into the rope of your marriage?

As a couple, write out a purpose statement for your marriage based upon the truths discussed in this session. Ask yourselves, *What is God's design for our marriage and how will it reflect to those around us the ultimate desire of God for oneness with His people?*

Have you ever made an open commitment to your spouse to place his or her needs above your own, upholding his or her interests and seeking his or her best?

Make that commitment now, and prayerfully ask God to help you maintain your commitments to love and respect one another and to submit to one another out of reverence for Christ.

the great *adventure*

God blessed them and said to them, "Be fruitful and increase in number;
fill the earth and subdue it. Rule over the fish of the sea and the birds of the air
and over every living creature that moves on the ground."
Genesis 1:28

I picture Adam and Eve in the Garden of Eden. They are young, alive with enthusiasm for the new world around them, daily discovering with delight the wonders of God's handiwork, marveling and rejoicing in the diverse beauty and intricate patterns of life around them. And it sounds like fun.

I, however, wake up, shower and dress, kiss my spouse and kids good-bye and head out for another day at work. I return home each evening and my "other" job begins: I clean or fix those things that need my attention, take care of the yards, pay the bills, help with homework—anything I can do to be a loving partner to my spouse and to be a good parent to my children.

Don't get me wrong—I love my life and all the challenges it brings. But in the hustle and bustle of daily life, I miss that raw pleasure of discovering the world around me. I forget that the same intricate beauty that awed Adam and Eve is at my fingertips too. Instead, every night, I pull the covers over my head, sleep a heavy sleep and prepare for another day.

The scenario I've just described is *not* what God intended. We miss the boat entirely if we think that He meant only for Adam and Eve to live in wide-eyed wonder at the world around them. God wants us, together as a man and woman joined by divine design, to enjoy a grand and wonder-filled existence. Like Adam and Eve, we were made to share a life marked by true awe of God's presence and power. So do we drop everything and run through fields of wild flowers until Jesus comes back? No. The greatest adventure we can experience as a couple is to surrender our lives and marriage to the will of God and labor together to see His purposes accomplished. From the smallest tasks we face to the greatest, God has given us a charge to work together for His glory.

1. List some of the jobs you have held.

2. Which one of your jobs was the most enjoyable? Why?

3. Which was the most difficult? Why?

4. Describe your perfect job.

5. Describe your spouse's perfect job.

God gave Adam and Eve the same job that He gives to each couple who has surrendered to His will. We were made to labor together in love. We weren't created to blindly run on the hamster wheel of our lives day in and day out—God wants us to awaken to life's great adventure!

planting the seed

Kids live for summer vacation—two months of freedom from work. They can hang out with friends, stay up late and not even *think* about homework, teachers and tests. Vacations are great; everyone needs time off from the routine to be refreshed—but living for our vacation time is not God's intention for us, and doing so only breeds discontentment and distress in our daily lives.

God wants us to see the work to which He calls us as a place of divine wonder and excitement. God created work; it was His idea. The labor to which He calls every living being is not a jail sentence to be endured but, rather, a chance to use gifts and talents we've been given in God-honoring and heart-satisfying service. Work is a gift. We labor both individually and as a couple with our ultimate goal being to enjoy God and bring Him glory.

6. According to Genesis 1:28 and 2:15, what was the work God called Adam and Eve to do?

It is important to note that God called both Adam and Eve to work together in these pursuits. Although we each have specific responsibilities, the major task set before us is still a joint effort, requiring the support and encouragement of both the husband and the wife.

Be Fruitful

God's first directive to Adam and Eve was to be fruitful. God expects the same from us today. Having been made in God's image, we are, by nature, creative beings—designed to be fruitful. But what does His command to be fruitful mean?

The logical conclusion we come to when we first think about God's command to reproduce is that it must mean having children. After all, we were made to be reproductive and creative beings who have been given the capacity to generate new life. However, some couples—whether by choice or circumstance—may not have children, but they can still be fruitful by bringing or guiding others into God's family. We are called not only to raise up children who serve and follow the Lord but also to allow God's grace to use our marriages to seed divine purpose into the lives of those around us. As instruments of grace, we are meant to touch others with God's divine blessing. As a couple united by God, you and your spouse are called to work together to reproduce God's blessings in the lives of friends and family.

7. Name two people who have had a positive spiritual impact on your life as a married couple. What did these people do that had such an impact?

8. How is God using your lives to touch those around you?

9. Name two people (besides your own children) whose lives you can impact as a couple.

10. How can you go about reaching out to these people?

Rule and Subdue

Adam and Eve had to rule over fish and frogs; we have computers and cars and jobs and budgets and sports and ministries and community service projects and quality family time—and the list goes on and on.

But stop and think for a minute about this command to rule. The earth was made for people to discover and enjoy—*and* to subdue. Now, more than ever, it seems that people are being subdued by the pressing needs around them, rather than subduing those needs and bringing them under control as God commanded. Subduing means simply bringing things under authority. Married couples must prioritize their lives so that everything is brought under the authority of the Scriptures.

11. List the activities in a typical week (including work) for you and your spouse.

12. Looking back over your list, what are the most important things you do in a week—things that make an eternal difference?

13. What could you change to see that these eternal values are more readily a part of your weekly routine?

Work and Upkeep

If you have ever planted a garden, you know the exhausting labor it requires: preparing the ground, devising a watering system, sowing the seed, etc. And just when you think everything is done, you realize that the work is not over—in fact, it *never* will be done!

A garden requires weeding, watering, feeding, pruning and cleaning up to keep it healthy and fruitful. Our lives, and especially our marriage relationships, need ongoing attention and care, too, or they can fall into dull routine that is as lifeless as it is unfruitful.

14. What do you do to encourage your walk with God daily? Weekly?

15. What do you do to cultivate your marriage relationship daily? Weekly?

The most relentless and destructive weeds in a marriage are lack of personal devotion to God, selfishness and failure to communicate well. The common strains of these weeds must be attentively watched for and plucked out as soon as they are noticed.

16. What are the weeds you have struggled with in your marriage?

17. What can you do to uproot these weeds?

No matter what our vocation, the charge is clear: Be fruitful, subdue the things that pull you away from devotion to God and to each other, and daily care for each other. Marriage is meant to be a shared adventure, a joyous and exciting journey of discovery of the amazing world God created for us. He wants us to walk together with Him! Dull routine was never part of the plan.

watering the hope

Laboring together takes the common bond that a husband and wife share through their marriage and adds to it a common purpose. Joined by divine design, knit together as one, marriage is a place of strength and security like no other relationship on Earth, a blessing to be relished and enjoyed. We can work together, laboring for God's purposes to be accomplished in us. When we subdue our schedules and tame our activities, we have the energy and ability to reach out to others with the love of God.

18. If married life is meant to be a great adventure, why does it so often seem to get stuck in a dull routine? What happens that leads a couple away from wide-eyed wonder and into stoic routine?

19. If a couple gets stuck in a routine, how can they become renewed with enthusiasm for God and for each other?

20. How has God used your life as a married couple to reflect His glory to others in your community?

Your church?

Your family?

21. What areas are your strong points as a married couple?

22. What areas are your weak points?

It is important to periodically take time to assess how God has specifically gifted both of you to serve others. Ask for His help as you order your lives so that His purposes are being accomplished in and through you as a couple and as individuals.

harvesting the fruit

The centerpiece of the Garden of Eden was the tree of life. This tree was the place where divine presence was as real as the fruit hanging from the trees. God wants His presence to be the centerpiece of our relationship and our work. Here's how it works.

- Work is a gift from God.
- We are called to labor together to accomplish God's will.
- Marriage is meant to be a place where God's purposes are worked out both individually and together.

23. How does knowing this divine order change your view of work?

24. Why did God appoint work for Adam and Eve instead of leaving them to merely enjoy His creation?

25. In what ways does work benefit us?

26. How does your spouse view his or her work?

How can you better support your spouse to accomplish the work God has given him or her to do?

Take a moment and pray together, asking God to renew your understanding of His purpose for you as a couple and to help you begin to see your lives as the great adventure He intends them to be.

Then begin each day this week by taking turns praying God's blessings over each other, specifically in the area of work and daily responsibility. Ask God for His presence to guide each of you and for His power to bless each of your efforts.

a walk
in the garden

Then the man and his wife heard the sound of the Lord God as he was walking in the garden in the cool of the day, and they hid from the Lord God among the trees of the garden. But the Lord God called to the man, "Where are you?"

Genesis 3:8-9

Tahiti, Maui, the French Riviera, Borneo, Cancun, Venice—these names communicate places of sun-drenched romanticism and carefree relaxation. Timeless places where we are certain that life itself must surely stand still, relinquishing its iron grip and yielding to a deeper enjoyment of living. Paradise!

1. Describe your idea of paradise—somewhere you would be content to live forever. What does it look like? What does it feel like?

2. What would your spouse describe as his or her paradise?

3. What is it about these places (real or imaginary) that makes them so desirable to each of you?

4. What is one thing that would ruin your paradise?

If any couple could have lived forever in paradise, it was Adam and Eve. They had a perfect world: a place God not only provided for them but in which He Himself walked and enjoyed His relationship with them.

So what happened? How could they be discontented in such a perfect place?

planting the seed

A major wireless service provider ran a series of ads in which the crucial part of an important conversation became lost or misunderstood because of screeching static. In one ad, just as the man was about to "pop the question" his voice was obscured by the sound of frantic scratching, not unlike running fingernails down a chalkboard. Needless to say, the conversation came to an abrupt halt. These ads tickled consumers' funny bones because everyone who uses modern technology—cell phones, computers or faxes—can identify with the failures that happen from time to time, usually when you least desire them.

This idea of static interruption is a fairly reasonable analogy to what happened in the Garden of Eden. Things were going well—*very* well. Adam and Eve enjoyed the beautiful creation around them with God Himself as their friend and teacher. They had everything they could ever want or need in this paradise—and more. But having everything didn't prevent Adam and Eve from disobeying God's command and severing that line of perfect communication with their maker. Sin introduces all kinds of static in our lives. It brings a screeching cry of selfishness and destruction that we cannot repair on our own. God's intention for us to become expressions of true oneness in Him has been obscured. So where do we go from here?

What Happened in the Garden?

Read the account of what happened in the Garden of Eden in Genesis 3:1-24.

5. What were the steps that the serpent took to deceive Eve (see vv. 1,4-5)?

6. How did Eve fall for his deception (see v. 6)?

7. In Genesis 3:5, what did the serpent say that God was withholding from Adam and Eve?

8. What happened when Adam and Eve ate the fruit (see v. 7)? Did they get what they wanted?

9. Although Adam tried to put the blame on Eve—and, ultimately, God (see v. 12)—what was his responsibility in the incident?

10. What were the results for Adam and Eve, as individuals and as a couple?

What *were* they thinking? It's easy to criticize them, but we shouldn't. The same thing happens to each of us too. We buy into a lie. It's as simple as that. We linger too long at the suggestion of the deceiver and become deceived. As a result, we seek our own interests and cease to acknowledge God as creator, king and friend.

Adam should have recognized the danger immediately and stepped in as the God-ordained ruler of the earth. After all, it was Adam who received the instructions from God and was therefore responsible for seeing that they were followed. Adam was commanded and gifted by God to rule the earth and to subdue it, yet by not asserting His God-given authority, he handed it over—and without a fight.

Eve should have questioned the serpent's words by going to Adam or even to God, who visited in the cool of the evening! After all, there had never before been a contradictory statement uttered in that paradise of Eden. Shouldn't that have raised a red flag?

So why didn't they do something? *Anything?* Because it requires courage to trust. At that point, when Adam could have had his greatest moment, he became a coward. And Eve did too. Given the opportunity to obey, even when she didn't fully understand, she caved and decided that the fruit—and what it would give her—was too good to pass up. No courage was displayed that day, only cowardice that cost them and their progeny everything.

11. In your marriage have you ever been tempted to do something, even though you knew that doing it would hurt your relationship? What happened?

The small, daily decisions we make can affect our relationships. Telling white lies, complaining about our spouse to others, continually bringing up our spouse's mistakes—all of these things can undermine a marriage relationship.

12. What are some things you can choose to pursue that might bring sorrow into your marriage?

What Happens to Us?

The Fall damaged our oneness. The incredible knitting of souls—the true one-flesh union—was altered and, instead, personal interest began to flourish, resulting in selfish thinking, *What about me?* Since the Fall, human beings have become inherently selfish. Selfishness in a marriage is like cancer in a body—it will result in death unless something happens to invite healing.

If personal happiness is our primary goal in our marriage, we will seek to gain it and resent anything or anyone who blocks our goal. The calling to become one necessitates that each one consider the other's desires and needs as more important. Jesus said that we are to love our neighbor—and this most certainly includes our spouse!—*as we love ourselves* (see Mark 12:31). The husband is told to love his wife as his own body (see Ephesians 5:28) and that "he who loves his wife loves himself" (Ephesians 5:29).

Every day there are situations in a marriage that force both husband and wife to confront their self-centeredness and choose instead to serve the other willingly and joyfully.

13. How do you put your spouse's needs before your own?

14. How does your spouse show you his or her willingness to put your desires and needs first?

15. In order to bless your spouse, what are ways in which you can sacrifice those things that you may want?

16. How does serving your spouse open the door to restoring God's original intention for marriage?

Thinking about Adam and Eve's experience, we can see that self-centered actions (i.e., choosing to ignore God's will and go our own way) produce less than what we desire.

17. During these selfish times, when did you realize that the problem might be in you or in your handling of a situation rather than with your spouse?

18. In what ways have you acted as the biggest obstacle to your own self-fulfillment?

19. What was the result?

The more we focus on our happiness through self-fulfilling desires, the less we are apt to discover what it is we *really* want. Serving others—especially our spouses—is God's way of throwing light on the path of our own success. It is in this way that happiness is not the purpose but the by-product of a healthy marriage, a marriage in the way God intended it to be.

Look over the following sample of how one spouse might have charted the high and low points in their marriage:

Marriage Chart (Sample)

	Year 1	Year 2	Year 3	Year 4	Year 5	Year 6	Year 7	Year 8	Year 9	Year 10
10	X		X							X
9		X							X	
8						X		X		
7							X			
6										
5				X						
4										
3										
2					X					
1										
*										

*In the spaces to the right, fill in the years, months (if married less than 3 years) or groups of years (if married more than 12 years).

Milestones in Our Marriage

Year 1: *Newly wedded bliss!*

Year 2: *Bought our condo—a little stressful, but worth it.*

Year 3: *An unexpected but welcome surprise!*

Year 4: *John laid off—decided to finish his degree and work part-time.*

Year 5: *A tough year financially—we ate lots of macaroni and cheese!*

Year 6: *John graduated school and the twins were born!*

Year 7: *A great new job offer and John's new career began.*

Year 8: *Baby number four arrived! Sold the condo and bought a house.*

Year 9: *Things began to smooth out financially.*

Year 10: *Renewed our vows and celebrated by taking a honeymoon cruise!*

Now chart your marriage in terms of its high and low points. Use the spaces provided to note the milestone events that triggered the high and low points.

Marriage Chart

10										
9										
8										
7										
6										
5										
4										
3										
2										
1										
*										

*In the spaces to the right, fill in the years, months (if married less than 3 years) or groups of years (if married more than 12 years).

Milestones in Our Marriage

———— : _____

———— : _____

———— : _____

———— : _____

———— : _____

———— : _____

———— : _____

———— : _____

———— : _____

———— : _____

Many couples feel that their marriage should be a continuous rise from glory to glory with total personal satisfaction and happiness enveloping every daily activity. But the reality is that marriage is a dynamic relationship that ebbs and flows through many seasons, some of which are wonderful and fulfilling and others that are exacting and frustrating.

But the common bond through it all is this: A husband and wife are joined by God in a unique bond and are suitable for each other. Life's ups and downs are meant to be places to draw closer together, to lean harder upon one another and the One who fashioned the bond between you and your spouse.

20. Describe a time when a difficulty worked to draw you closer to your spouse.

21. How did God work in that circumstance to strengthen your relationship?

What Can We Do Now?

As we can see in the results of the Fall as recorded in Genesis 3, sin distances us in our relationships and damages our ability to enjoy marriage as God intended. This is bound to bring up feelings of guilt over past failures in our relationships. Don't linger there and allow the deceiver to keep you locked in the past. God has provided full redemption for you.

The only way out of the pain caused by sin is to admit the failure. When we confess our sin, we can receive forgiveness and get our lives back in right order. God, who loves His creation more than we could ever understand, knew what would happen when the serpent finally found a chance to talk to Eve. He knew that Adam would join her in committing sin and that God's perfect design for their lives with God would be altered forever. But God had a plan.

22. Write out 1 John 1:9.

Every person has areas of weakness and will fail from time to time, allowing the static of sin to creep back in, cluttering the intentions of God for our well-being and growth. The answer is to lay our weaknesses at the foot of the cross before the Christ who bore our sin in His own flesh.

23. According to Isaiah 53:3-5 and 1 Peter 2:24, what did Jesus Christ bear so that we might be freed from our debt of sin?

Surrendering your weaknesses and frailties to God allows Him to pour His grace into you. Weakness is not a shame or a defect; it is an opportunity to make an honest assessment of yourself and to invite God to fill the gaps and strengthen the bond between you and your spouse.

24. What does 2 Corinthians 12:9 say about weakness?

25. What has been the most challenging area of weakness in your marriage?

26. What specific ways can you invite God's grace into that area of weakness?

27. How did the Fall affect the marriage relationship?

28. In what ways have you seen selfishness creep into your own marriage relationship?

29. Explain why you agree or disagree with the following statement: If marriage is about personal happiness, then it is justifiable to divorce when you are no longer happy.

30. How does placing your spouse's desires and needs above your own provide a way for you to experience personal fulfillment?

harvesting the fruit

After God created Adam and Eve, He didn't leave them to fend for themselves. He walked *with* them in the Garden of Eden, meaning for this three-way relationship to be the couple's source of daily strength and guidance.

It is likewise for us: God doesn't just join us to our spouse in marriage and then leave us to work out the particulars on our own. He designed a marriage relationship to include Himself. Each marriage partner needs the ongoing infusion of God's presence to grow more intimate, not only with each other, but also with the Lord.

It would be great if the story had ended something like this: Adam and Eve enjoyed their daily visits with God, growing in their understanding of His ways and of nature through the creation around them, while deepening their own love and union in the process.

Unfortunately, the sin of Adam and Eve stole this amazing gift, and its effects have filtered down to every human life and relationship since then. Because of their sin, our three-way relationship with God was marred and needed the redemption that could only be found through the sacrifice of the lamb, our redeemer, Jesus Christ.

Through Jesus' death for our sins and His resurrection, God provided a way out of this mess and we can once again walk with God in intimate relationship—both as individuals and as a couple.

Choose a time this week to serve communion to each other. Read through the following passages; then as you partake of the bread and the wine (or grape juice), remember that God has committed Himself to you and your spouse, both as individuals and as a couple—and it is His desire to see you succeed.

- Matthew 26:26-29
- Mark 14:22-24
- Luke 22:19-20
- 1 Corinthians 11:23-25

After sharing communion, take turns praying for each other and praising God for bringing you together in His ultimate wisdom and plan.

1. *leader's* discussion guide

General Guidelines

1. If at all possible, the group should be led by a married couple. This does not mean that both spouses need to be leading the discussions; perhaps one spouse is better at facilitating discussions while the other is better at relationship building or organization—but the leader couple should share responsibilities wherever possible.

2. At the first meeting, be sure to lay down the ground rules for discussions, stressing that following these rules will help everyone feel comfortable during discussion times.

   a. No one should share anything of a personal or potentially embarrassing nature without first asking his or her spouse's permission.

   b. Whatever is discussed in the group meetings is to be held in strictest confidence among group members only.

   c. Allow everyone in the group to participate. However, as a leader, don't force anyone to answer a question if he or she is reluctant. Be sensitive to the different personalities and communication styles among your group members.

3. Fellowship time is very important in building small-group relationships. Providing beverages and/or light refreshments either before or after each session will encourage a time of informal fellowship.

4. Most people live very busy lives; respect the time of your group members by beginning and ending meetings on time.

The Focus on the Family Marriage Ministry Guide *has even more information on starting and leading a small group. You will find this an invaluable resource as you lead others through this Bible study.*

How to Use the Material

1. Each session has more than enough material to cover in a 45-minute teaching period. You will probably not have time to discuss every single question in each session, so prepare for each meeting by selecting questions you feel are most important to address for your group; discuss other questions as time permits. Be sure to save the last 10 minutes of your meeting time for each couple to interact individually and to pray together before adjourning.

    Optional Eight-Session Plan—You can easily divide each session into two parts if you'd like to cover all of the material presented in each session. Each section of the session has enough questions to divide in half, and the Bible study sections (Planting the Seed) are divided into two or three sections that can be taught in separate sessions.

2. Each spouse should have his or her own copy of the book in order to personally answer the questions. The general plan of this study is that the couples complete the questions at home during the week and then bring their books to the meeting to share what they have learned during the week.

    However, the reality of leading small groups in this day and age is that some members will find it difficult to do the homework. If you find that to be the case with your group, consider adjusting the lessons and having members complete the study during your meeting time as you guide them through the lesson. If you use this method, be sure to encourage members to share their individual answers with their spouses during the week (perhaps on a date night).

Session One | Great Expectations

*A **Note to Leaders:** This Bible study series is based on* The Marriage Masterpiece[1] *by Al Janssen. We highly recommend that you read the prologue and chapters 1 through 5 in preparation for leading this study.*

Before the Meeting

1. Gather materials for making name tags (if couples do not already know each other and/or if you do not already know everyone's name). Also gather extra pens or pencils and Bibles to use as loaners for anyone who needs them.

2. Make photocopies of the Prayer Request Form (see *The Focus on the Family Marriage Ministry Guide,* "Reproducible Forms" section) or provide 3x5-inch index cards for recording requests.

3. Read through your own answers and mark the ones that you especially want to have the group discuss.

4. Prepare slips of paper with the references for the verses that you will want someone to read aloud during the sessions. (For example, Planting the Seed's question 9, you may want to have some members read the verses listed before they share what the verses say about hope.) You can pass out these slips as members arrive, but be sensitive to those who are uncomfortable reading aloud or who might not be familiar with the Bible.

Ice Breakers

1. If this is the first time this couples group has met together, have everyone introduce themselves and tell a little bit about the amount of time they have been married, where they were married, etc.

2. Invite couples to share a funny thing that happened at their wedding or a how-we-met story.

3. **Option**—Have members share their answers to question 1 in Tilling the Ground (p. 12)—about their childhood expectations of marriage.

Discussion

1. **Tilling the Ground**—Begin the discussion by inviting volunteers to share their answers to some of the questions. (Questions 1, 2, 5 and 6 are probably best for group discussion. Be sensitive to the time, as you will want to spend most of your discussion time on the next two sections: the Bible study and application.)

2. **Planting the Seed**—Lead the group through the Bible study discussion, briefly reviewing the commentary as transitions between the questions. Refrain from reading the commentary word for word, except where necessary for clarity.

3. **Watering the Hope**—The questions in this section will help members bring the Bible study into the reality of their own expectations versus God's plan. Don't neglect this part of the study, as it bring the whole lesson into the here and now, applying God's Word to each member's daily life.

4. **Harvesting the Fruit**—This section is meant to help the individual couples apply the lesson to their own marriages and can be dealt with in several ways.

   a. Allow the couples one-on-one time at the end of the meeting. This would require space for them to be alone, with enough space between couples to allow for quiet, private conversations.

   If couples have already answered the questions individually, now would be the time to share their answers. Give a time limit, emphasizing that their discussions can be continued at home if they are not able to answer all of the questions in the time allotted.

   If couples have not answered the questions before the meeting, have them answer them together now. This works best when there is open-ended time for the couples to stay until they have completed their discussion and will require that the leaders stay until the last couple has finished.

   b. Instruct couples to complete this section at home during the week after the meeting. This will give them quiet and private time to deal with any issues that might come up and to spend all the time needed to complete the discussion. You will want to follow up at the next meeting to hold couples accountable for completing this part of the lesson.

c. At times it might be advantageous to pair up couples to discuss these questions. This would help in building accountability into the study.

5. **Close in Prayer**—An important part of any small-group relationship is the time spent in prayer for one another. This may also be done in a number of ways.

   a. Have couples write out their specific prayer requests on the Prayer Request Forms (or index cards). These requests may then be shared with the whole group or traded with another couple as prayer partners for the week. If requests are shared with the whole group, pray as a group before adjourning the meeting; if requests are traded, allow time for the prayer-partner couples to pray together.

   b. Gather the whole group together and lead couples in guided prayer, asking that God will continue to open their eyes to His plan for their marriage.

   c. Have individual couples pray together.

After the Meeting

1. **Evaluate**—Leaders should spend time evaluating the meeting's effectiveness (see *The Focus on the Family Marriage Ministry Guide*, "Reproducible Forms" section, for an evaluation form).

2. **Encourage**—During the week, try to contact each couple (through phone calls, notes of encouragement or e-mail/instant messaging) and welcome them to the group. Make yourself available for answering any questions or concerns they may have and generally get to know them. This contact might best be done by the husband-leader contacting the men and the wife-leader contacting the women.

3. **Equip**—Complete the Bible study, even if you have previously gone through this study together.

4. **Pray**—Prayerfully prepare for the next meeting, praying for each couple and for your own preparation.

Reminder: In your desire to serve the members of your group, don't neglect your own marriage. Spend quality time with your spouse during the week!

Session Two | The Divine Triangle

Before the Meeting

1. Gather several Bibles, pens or pencils, and the materials needed to make name tags.
2. Make photocopies of the Prayer Request Form or provide 3x5-inch index cards for recording requests.
3. Read through your own answers and mark the ones that you especially want to have the group discuss.
4. Prepare slips of paper with the references for the verses that you will want someone to read aloud during the session. (You can distribute these slips as members arrive.)
5. Obtain three contrasting-colored spools of sewing thread (e.g., red, white and blue). Cut the threads into 18-inch lengths, enough to make a set of six pieces (two of each color) for each couple in your group.

Ice Breakers

1. As couples arrive, give each a prepared set of threads and instruct them to place the threads carefully—so they don't tangle—in their study book or Bible until the meeting begins.
2. Distribute Prayer Request Forms (or index cards) and ask members to at least write down their name, even if they don't have a specific prayer request. This way, another couple can pray for them during the upcoming week. (After all, just because we don't have a specific request doesn't mean we don't need prayer!)
3. Invite volunteers to share how they applied to their marriage relationship what they learned in last week's session. Here are some suggested questions to ask:
   a. How did a better understanding of God's expectation for marriage give you a strong point of hope for your relationship?
   b. How did your marriage relationship reflect something of God's nature and/or give glory to Him during this week?
   c. What is one thing that you learned in last week's meeting that helped you understand (or illustrate) God's plan for marriage?

Discussion

1. **Tilling the Ground**—Begin the meeting with an object lesson followed by a discussion. (**Note:** Be sure to practice the object lesson before the meeting!)

   a. Instruct each husband to take the blue thread (or whatever color you choose) and have the wife try to break it—which will be very easy to do. Then have the wives each take a red and white thread and hold them together while the husbands try to break them. Again, this should be fairly easy to do (unless you've chosen industrial-strength thread!) Finally, instruct the couples to take the remaining three threads and with each spouse holding opposite ends of the threads, twist them. When the threads have been twisted together, ask the husbands to try to break the "cord of three strands." It should be impossible (or nearly so) to do.

   b. Begin the discussion by inviting a volunteer to read Ecclesiastes 4:12 and then have those who wish to do so share their answers to questions 1 and 2.

2. **Planting the Seed**—Discuss questions 3 through 7.

   a. "Strengthening the Strands" and "Great Marriages Begin with Personal Commitments to Jesus Christ" may be skipped if you are sure all of the group members have made personal commitments to Christ; however, don't assume this is the case. Instead you can simply ask if anyone has questions about this section and if any decisions were made. Be sensitive to those in your group that may have recently made, or might be ready to make, a commitment to Jesus Christ. Invite members to talk to you afterwards if they have recently made or are now ready to make a decision for Christ.

   b. "Great Marriages Are Strengthened by Consistent Personal Devotion" questions 13 through 15 can be covered fairly quickly. Question 16 is a personal question that individuals need to answer for themselves.

   c. "Great Marriages Endure Through Ongoing Personal Submission" will more than likely provide the most lively discussion of this session. There are also several personal-application questions in this section; it might be best to leave the personal questions for the couple to discuss alone. Those questions reflecting on the biblical basis of personal submission will provide enough material for group discussion.

3. **Watering the Hope**—For this discussion divide the group by gender. The wives will discuss question 25, and the husbands will discuss question 26.

   a. After the groups have had a few minutes to discuss their question, challenge the men and women to keep each other accountable to showing submission "to one another out of reverence for Christ" (Ephesians 5:21) and then have the two groups pray for one another.

   b. Encourage the men to call each other during the week and ask how they are doing in showing love to their wives. Encourage the women to call one another and ask how they are doing in showing respect for their husbands. You can also have members pair up with a same-sex accountability partner for the coming week.

4. **Harvesting the Fruit**—Have spouses pair up and share their answers to questions 27 through 33. Assign the project of writing their marriage purpose statement during the week and let them know they will be asked to read their statements at next week's meeting.

5. **Close in Prayer**—Have couples pray together following the direction at the end of the session. As couples leave, have members each select someone else's Prayer Request Form (or index card) so that they can pray for that person during the coming week.

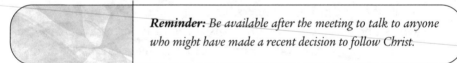

Reminder: Be available after the meeting to talk to anyone who might have made a recent decision to follow Christ.

After the Meeting

1. **Evaluate.**
2. **Encourage** accountability partners to call one another during the week to see how each is doing in honoring his or her spouse.
3. **Equip.**
4. **Pray.**

Session Three | The Great Adventure

Before the Meeting

1. Gather index cards, pens or pencils, and Bibles, as needed.
2. Make photocopies of the Prayer Request Form or provide 3x5-inch index cards for recording requests.
3. Read through your own answers and mark the ones that you especially want to have the group discuss.
4. Prepare slips of paper with the references for the verses that you will want someone to read aloud during the session. (You can distribute these slips as members arrive.)

Ice Breakers

1. Distribute index cards as members arrive and tell them to write their first names on their cards and also write what they as children dreamed that they would be when they grew up. Instruct everyone to keep their cards to themselves, not even sharing what they've written with their spouses.
2. When everyone has had enough time to write their childhood dream, collect the cards and mix up their order. Starting with the top card, read the dream and ask the group to guess to whom the dream belongs.

Discussion

1. **Tilling the Ground**—Begin the meeting by asking couples to read their marriage purpose statements.
   a. Ask members to briefly share the worst or the best job they have ever held.
   b. Invite volunteers to describe their dream job.
2. **Planting the Seed**—Discuss the questions.
3. **Watering the Hope**—Have each couple partner with another to discuss questions 18 through 20. Instruct couples to share the strengths they see in the partner couple's marriage.

4. **Harvesting the Fruit**—Have spouses share with each other their answers to questions 23 through 26. Challenge couples to begin to discover the work that God has planned for them to do together.

5. **Close in Prayer**—Have each couple partner with another again to share what each has written on his or her Prayer Request Form (or index card). Once they've shared, have them pray together.

After the Meeting

1. **Evaluate.**
2. **Encourage** the prayer-partner couples to contact one another during the week to share answers to prayer.
3. **Equip.**
4. **Pray.**

Session Four | A Walk in the Garden

Before the Meeting

1. Provide pens or pencils and Bibles, as needed.
2. Make photocopies of the Study Review Form (see *The Focus on the Family Marriage Ministry Guide*, "Reproducible Forms" section).
3. Make photocopies of the Prayer Request Form or provide 3x5-inch index cards for recording requests.
4. Read through your own answers and mark the ones that you especially want to have the group discuss.
5. Prepare slips of paper with the references for the verses that you will want someone to read aloud during the session. (You can distribute these slips as members arrive.)
6. Gather several travel posters of desirable vacation spots around the world and attach the posters to the walls around the meeting room. (If you are unable to find travel posters, make signs with the names of vacation spots using poster board and felt-tip pens.)
7. If you are providing the communion elements for the optional closing activity, prepare these beforehand.

Ice Breakers

1. Invite members to look at the posters scattered around the room and select the one that best describes their favorite (or dream) vacation spot. Have them share their reason for selecting that spot.
2. Have members describe their idea of paradise.

Discussion

1. **Tilling the Ground**—Discuss questions 1, 3 and 4.
2. **Planting the Seed**—Instruct members to close their eyes and imagine what it must have been like to be in the Garden of Eden, at peace and at one with God and each other. Have them continue to keep their eyes closed as you read Genesis 2:4-25 aloud. Invite volunteers to share what they pictured as you read.
   a. Have a volunteer read Genesis 3:1-24. Discuss questions 5 through 10.

b. Most of the questions (13 through 21) in "What Happens to Us?" are intended for self-evaluation. You may want to allow time after the group discussion for members to reflect on their answers to these questions; otherwise suggest that they prayerfully do so at home during the week. The chart section could be discussed as a couple during Harvesting the Fruit or at home during the week.

b. Continue the group discussion with questions 22 through 27.

3. **Watering the Hope**—Have each couple partner with another to discuss this section's questions.

4. **Harvesting the Fruit**—There are two possible ways to end this session.

a. Have couples discuss their answers to questions 13 through 21, especially the chart and the questions immediately following. Then close in prayer.

b. Provide the elements for individual couples to celebrate communion together. If you do not provide communion elements at this time, urge couples to celebrate communion at home during the week.

5. **Close in Prayer**—Ask group members to stand in a circle, and allow time for sentence prayers of praise and worship. Close by singing a worship song together.

After the Meeting

1. **Evaluate**—Distribute the Study Review Forms for members to take home with them. Share the importance of feedback, and ask members to take the time this week to write their review of the group meetings and then to return them to you.

2. **Encourage**—Call each couple during the next week and invite them to join you for the next study in the *Focus on the Family Marriage Series*.

Note

1. Al Janssen, *The Marriage Masterpiece* (Wheaton, IL: Tyndale House Publishers, 2001).

Welcome to the Family!

As you participate in the *Focus on the Family Marriage Series*, it is our prayerful hope that God will deepen your understanding of His plan for marriage and that He will strengthen your marriage relationship.

This series is just one of the many helpful, insightful, and encouraging resources produced by Focus on the Family. In fact, that's what Focus on the Family is all about—providing inspiration, information, and biblically based advice to people in all stages of life.

It began in 1977 with the vision of one man, Dr. James Dobson, a licensed psychologist and author of 18 best-selling books on marriage, parenting, and family. Alarmed by the societal, political, and economic pressures that were threatening the existence of the American family, Dr. Dobson founded Focus on the Family with one employee and a once-a-week radio broadcast aired on only 36 stations.

Now an international organization, the ministry is dedicated to preserving Judeo-Christian values and strengthening and encouraging families through the life-changing message of Jesus Christ. Focus ministries reach families worldwide through 10 separate radio broadcasts, two television news features, 13 publications, 18 Web sites, and a steady series of books and award-winning films and videos for people of all ages and interests.

We'd love to hear from you!

For more information about the ministry, or if we can be of help to your family, simply write to Focus on the Family, Colorado Springs, CO 80995 or call 1-800-A-FAMILY (1-800-232-6459). Friends in Canada may write Focus on the Family, P.O. Box 9800, Stn. Terminal, Vancouver, B.C. V6B 4G3 or call 1-800-661-9800. Visit our Web site— www.family.org—to learn more about Focus on the Family or to find out if there is an associate office in your country.

Strengthen and enrich your marriage with these Focus on the Family® relationship builders.

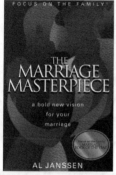

The Marriage Masterpiece
Now that you've discovered the richness to be had in "The Focus on the Family Marriage Series" Bible studies, be sure to read the book the series is based on. *The Marriage Masterpiece* takes a fresh appraisal of the exquisite design God has for a man and woman. Explaining the reasons why this union is meant to last a lifetime, it also shows how God's relationship with humanity is the model for marriage. Rediscover the beauty and worth of marriage in a new light with this thoughtful, creative book. A helpful study guide is included for group discussion. Hardcover.

The Love List
Marriage experts Drs. Les and Leslie Parrot present eight healthy habits that refresh, transform and restore the intimacy of your marriage relationship. Filled with practical suggestions, this book will help you make daily, weekly, monthly and yearly improvements in your marriage. Hardcover.

Capture His Heart/Capture Her Heart
Lysa TerKeurst has written two practical guides—one for wives and one for husbands—that will open your eyes to the needs, desires and longings of your spouse. These two books each offer eight essential criteria plus creative tips for winning and holding his or her heart. Paperback set.

• • •

Look for these special books in your Christian bookstore or request a copy by calling 1-800-A-FAMILY (1-800-232-6459). Friends in Canada may write Focus on the Family, P.O. Box 9800, Stn. Terminal, Vancouver, B.C. V6B 4G3 or call 1-800-661-9800.

Visit our Web site (www.family.org) to learn more about the ministry or find out if there is a Focus on the Family office in your country.